BBC MUSIC GUIDES

MOZART CHAMBER MUSIC

BBC MUSIC GUIDES

General editor: GERALD ABRAHAM

BBC MUSIC GUIDES

Mozart Chamber Music

A. HYATT KING

BRITISH BROADCASTING CORPORATION

Published by the British Broadcasting Corporation
35 Marylebone High Street, London, W.1

SBN: 563 07307 1

First published 1968

© A. Hyatt King 1968

Printed in England by
Billing & Sons Limited, Guildford and London

CONTENTS

Acknowledgements

Passages from *The Letters of Mozart and his Family*, translated and edited by Emily Anderson (second edition, 1966, by A. Hyatt King and Monica Carolan) are quoted by kind permission of Messrs Macmillan & Co. Grateful acknowledgement is also due to Messrs A. & C. Black for passages quoted from *Mozart: A documentary biography*, by O. E. Deutsch, translated by Eric Blom, Peter Branscombe, and Jeremy Noble; and to Bärenreiter-Verlag for the excerpt from E. F. Schmid's edition of Mozart's String Quintet in D.

Introduction

'Storace gave a quartett party to his friends. The players were tolerable; not one of them excelled on the instrument he played, but there was a little science among them, which I dare say will be acknowledged when I name them:

> The First Violin   Haydn
> The Second Violin   Baron Dittersdorf
> The Violoncello   Vanhall
> The Tenor   Mozart

The poet Casti and Paesiello formed part of the audience. I was there, and a greater treat, or a more remarkable one, cannot be imagined.'

This passage, from the *Reminiscences* of Michael Kelly (who sang Don Basilio in the first production of *Figaro*), suggests one reason why Mozart's chamber works form such a vital and endlessly fascinating part of his music: he lost no opportunity of taking part in a performance himself. We may be sure that he did so on many more occasions than on those of which we have record, because playing meant nearly as much to him as composing. The one illuminated and inspired the other. Despite Mozart's gifts as a pianist, his favourite instrument was the viola – appropriately enough, for it lies at the heart of the string quartet. It is the quartets, no less than their wonderful companion pieces, the string quintets on the one hand and the string duos and the string trio on the other, that contain the essence of his greatness as a composer of chamber music. As these pages will show, Mozart wrote many other fine works, often highly original in timbre and choice of instruments, and most moving to hear, but it was through the medium of stringed instruments alone that he, like Haydn and Beethoven, sought to express some of his most profound feelings.

For the purpose of this booklet, the term 'chamber music' – difficult to define at any period – will exclude Mozart's serenades, divertimenti and the various wind pieces written for masonic occasions, but will include all his other compositions intended for informal, domestic performance with but one player to each part. (The number of his chamber works known to have been written primarily for a public audience is very small.) Mozart composed his chamber music for sundry reasons: to attract or flatter an influential patron; to extend his reputation, or to make a little money by fulfilling a commission from a publisher or a wealthy amateur; to please or help a friend; to repay a debt or express gratitude; to provide a distinguished player with a new piece.

We can better appreciate the fullness of Mozart's achievement if we understand something of the condition of chamber music in the earlier part of the eighteenth century. Since about 1660, its most popular form had been the trio-sonata which had been fostered in Italy by Legrenzi, Corelli, Vitali and Locatelli and had spread rapidly beyond the Alps. It was written for two melody instruments, usually violins, but sometimes oboes or flutes, with a figured bass for harpsichord, sometimes supported by a stringed bass, originally a violone, later a cello. Between about 1730 and 1750, the figured bass became obsolescent, and the harpsichord gradually dropped out, partly because it was too cumbrous to be transported easily into the open air where it became fashionable for the newer forms of music, divertimenti, notturni and cassations, to be played. The structure of these pieces, a loosely strung sequence of movements in varying tempi, was as diverse as the combination of instruments used. Gradually, there emerged a pattern of three movements, two in fairly quick tempo flanking a slower one, and when the minuet was added, the ultimate form of the string quartet took shape.

Its constituent instruments were established when, about 1745, the viola joined the popular group of two violins and a cello which had survived the dissolution of the trio-sonata. These results were achieved only after a period of ferment and experiment which also produced new ideas of musical expression and style as the baroque tradition disintegrated. While many composers in many parts of Europe made important contributions, it was largely in such progressive centres of musical activity as Mannheim and Vienna that the foundations of classical chamber music were laid. The greatest contribution of all came from the work of Franz Joseph Haydn whose slowly maturing genius became identified with purposeful perfecting of the string quartet.[1] Much as Mozart owed to the many composers whose music he heard during his

[1] This is described in another 'BBC Music Guide', *Haydn String Quartets*, by Rosemary Hughes (1966).

early travels, his greatest debt was to Haydn. Without his work, Mozart's progress towards mastery of the quartet and other forms would have been slower and more hesitant. He was fortunate in his generation, because he was not naturally a patient discoverer, but rather one who assimilated the ideas of others and reshaped and expanded them to contain the force of his restless genius.

1. The Early Violin Sonatas, 1762–6

Mozart's three earliest groups of chamber works were composed during the first of his strenuous European tours. The four sonatas for piano and violin, K. 6, 7, and K. 8, 9, date from 1762 to 1764, and were all published in Paris. They were followed by a set of six sonatas, K. 10–15, each with a cello ad libitum, composed in London and published there in 1765. The last set of these juvenile pieces is the six violin sonatas, K. 26–31, written and published at the Hague in 1766. In all these the violin usually does little more than play in thirds or sixths with the treble of the keyboard and, occasionally, in imitation of it. The cello, when present, hugs the safety of the bass. There are occasional sparks of originality, as in the fine and rather rhetorical violin part in the *andante* of K. 15, but the boy was generally less adventurous than some of his models, who included Schobert, J. C. Bach and Abel.

2. The Early String Quartets, 1770–3

Rather strangely, Mozart wrote no more violin sonatas for over twelve years. During this period his incessant cultivation of larger forms left him little time for chamber music, and he devoted it entirely to the string quartet. While all the juvenile sonatas were dedicated, under his father's guidance, to royal personages, none of the first thirteen quartets bore any dedication at all. They were all written to satisfy his youthful urge to explore this most intimate of musical forms.

He seems to have felt that the first (K. 80, in G) was something of a landmark in his creative life. For the autograph bears what is, for this date, an unusually full inscription: 'Quarteto di Amadeo Wolfgango Mozart, a Lodi 1770 le 15 di Marzo alle 7. di sera.' Eight years later, when writing to his father, he recalled that the quartet was composed at an inn. It was in fact where they stayed during their memorable first journey in Italy, on the way from Milan to Bologna. At Milan Mozart first heard the quartets of the aged Sammartini whose style, while fresh and melodious, was still largely based on the trio sonata. But this music made a lively impression on Mozart, whose little quartet originally consisted of three movements only, in the Italian manner, all very short and in the same key. The melodic and structural interest lies entirely in the two violins: the viola has a slender role and the cello still retains much of the character of a continuo part, as the following example shows:

EX. I

The fourth movement – a mere sixty-seven bars, which, however, include a coda – was added in 1773 or 1774. It is naturally more mature and rather less Italianate than the first three movements.

Three divertimenti, K. 135, 136 and 137, composed early in 1772 at Salzburg, are included in the Breitkopf edition of the string quartets. But the title 'divertimento', though found at the head of each autograph, is not in Mozart's hand, and the instrumentation specifies violas. This, and the fact that none of them has a minuet, suggests that these are really short symphonies, rather than quartets.

Mozart's first group of six quartets dates from the time of his third journey to north Italy, in the winter of 1772 to 1773, when he was still only sixteen. He wrote the first of the six at Bolzano – a place he detested – and the rest at Milan, where the great event was the composition and production of his opera *Lucio Silla*. While the style of the quartets is still Italianate, they show, rather better than most of his other works of this period, the growth of his musical personality. His liking for minor keys in the second movements is unusual. Above all, he began to feel his way towards true chamber music. In the first quartet, K. 155, in D, there is much that is fresh and delightful – but also still a good deal of padding. In general, the second violin and viola have distinctive parts, especially in the development of the first movement. In the opening *presto* of the second quartet, K. 156, in G, the music pulsates with the sheer joy of creation. Here too the development is remarkable:

EX. 2

The *adagio*, in E minor, cost Mozart some trouble. He discarded a twenty-four-bar beginning in favour of a movement with rather more individual roles for the lower strings. The C major quartet, K. 157, is notable for its unusual symmetry – each of the three movements is 126 bars long – and for the poignancy of its C minor *andante*. Again, in the fourth quartet, K. 158, in F, the slow movement, in A minor, is the most striking of the three: it has some nice touches of canon. In the B flat quartet, K. 159, the second movement is, exceptionally, an *allegro*. It is in G minor, and shows clearly the evocative power that this key already held for Mozart. Such a passage as this seems to foreshadow his later use of it:

EX. 3

In the sixth quartet in E flat, K. 160, one wonders if Mozart perhaps paid Haydn a conscious tribute in writing an opening melody that is virtually identical with that of the second phrase of the *adagio* of the latter's first quartet, Op. 1, no. 1.

Whether Mozart actually studied Haydn's early quartets, Op. 1 to Op. 9, seems uncertain. But there is little doubt that during the five or six months separating the completion of K. 155–160 from the next group of six, Mozart became acquainted, while on his third visit to Vienna, with Haydn's Op. 17 and Op. 20. It was the latter, published in 1772 as the 'Sun' quartets, which made the deeper impression. In these serious works, remarkable for their depth and range of feeling, Haydn sometimes moved so far away from the *galant* style that he composed four of the six finales as fugues. Mozart, at seventeen, seems to have found the masterful example of the older composer, then forty, rather disconcerting. Although he paid Haydn the sincere compliment of imitation, the result was a somewhat uneasy mixture of styles in which his later command of subtle contrast was still lacking. But throughout these six quartets, the increasingly free writing for all four instruments shows how fast Mozart was approaching maturity.

Here too, as with K. 80,[1] Mozart seems to have been conscious of an important stage in his development. That he conceived the six works as a group is shown by the heading of the autograph which reads '6 Quartetti del Sigr: Cav. Amadeo Wolfgango Mozart, a Vienna 1773 nel mese d'Agosto'. In the first movement of K. 168, in F, he shows his adroit, if limited, handling of a thematic device which he used later with more elaborate skill. He takes for development not the whole of the three-bar opening theme (remarkably like that of Haydn's Op. 17, no. 3), but only the third bar, and amplifies it most effectively. The *andante*, in F minor (played with mutes throughout), opens with a four-part canon and shows that Mozart can now write with ease sustained counterpoint in which all four parts are equally important. Here too he is indebted to Haydn, for the theme strongly resembles that of the latter's Op. 20, no. 5. The fugal finale is skilfully constructed but rather lacking in contrast.

The third work, K. 170, in C, is distinguished by an opening *adagio* comprising a theme and variations, the first in any Mozart quartet. It is of the simple melismatic type. A similar kind of accompanied cantilena is found in the slow movement. The fourth quartet, in E flat, K. 171, is altogether bolder and more distinctive. The first movement opens with a fine *adagio* of fourteen bars, introductory to an *allegro* with a fugal tinge, which is rounded off by the unexpected return of the *adagio* with subtle modifications. The *andante* (with mutes) is a surprisingly serious and contrapuntal piece in C minor: it was probably planned in deliberate contrast to the finale, which is a gay conception, in sonata form, with fanciful, lilting melodies in 3/8 time.

The B flat quartet, K. 172, is on the whole superficial, and the least personal of the set. There is perhaps a touch of Haydn in the treatment of the second subject of the first movement which Mozart gives to the two violins playing in octave unison. The *adagio* is a charming cantilena for the first violin, with broken figuration, anticipatory of many later works, for the other instruments. In the minuet, Mozart ventures into a contrapuntal style then uncommon for this movement. The sixth quartet, K. 173, in

[1] After the first mention of a work, with title, key and Köchel number, it will be referred to by K. number only. A list of works, in this order, is given on pp. 67–8.

D minor, is altogether a more serious affair. Its first movement is virtually dominated by the second subject – eleven repetitions of the same note with a trill in the middle – which runs through many different keys. The slow movement is in D major, a rather unusual key-relationship. It has an easy, flowing melody, but the minuet, in D minor, is formal and rather stern, without much concession to traditional grace. For the finale, Mozart wrote a strict fugue on a long descending chromatic subject which he treated with such elaborate skill that it seems as if he wanted to end this set of quartets by showing the musicians of Vienna how completely he had mastered the art of counterpoint.

The effect of this group as a whole is rather ambiguous. At its best, the free handling of the parts leaves no doubt that Mozart had developed technical mastery in this medium. But he had found it difficult to assimilate all the niceties and innovations of Haydn's music. The effort which the attempt cost him is manifest in a certain lack of balance in each quartet as a whole. It is in the non-fugal pieces that Mozart finds musical expression that is true to himself. Pressure of other work kept him away from the string quartet for just over nine years, a period which, by an odd coincidence, is almost exactly the same as the interval separating Haydn's quartets Op. 20 from his Op. 33.

3. Works for Strings and a Wind Instrument, 1775-82

During this long gap Mozart wrote a considerable number of sonatas and other pieces for piano and violin (which may best be considered later in the context of his mature masterpieces in this form) and six works in each of which a wind instrument predominates. These latter, lying as they do rather outside the main stream of Mozart's development in true chamber music, can appropriately be discussed here.

The Sonata for bassoon and cello, K. 292, usually assigned on stylistic and circumstantial grounds to the beginning of 1775, was probably written in Munich for Baron Thaddeus von Dürnitz, an amateur of the instrument. The bassoon's part is admirably composed to show off all its expressive powers, while the cello plays a subordinate, but by no means uninteresting role as an accompaniment, with some pleasant touches of imitation. Three of the four quartets for flute and strings were likewise the result of a commission – from a wealthy Dutchman named in Mozart's letters as 'De Jean', whom he met in Mannheim in the winter of 1777–8. (As 'De Jean' is plainly a corruption, it has been conjectured that this patron is identical with Willem Van Britten Dejong, to whom Dittersdorf dedicated a symphony at about this time.) In all these three quartets, the style is 'concertante', with the three strings mostly playing an accompaniment rather than taking part in a dialogue on equal terms. In the first, K. 285, in D, dated 25 December 1777, there are many delicate touches, especially in the very beautiful B minor *adagio*: its thirty-five bars are one of the most moving elegies written for the instrument. Music of this quality makes one wonder if Mozart really disliked the flute as much as he is reputed to have done. The concluding rondo, with its gay, varied treatment of the main theme and dancing appogiaturas, comes nearer to true chamber music. The other quartets, K. 285a, in G, and K. 285b, in C, both written early in 1778, are each of two movements only, and are of slighter interest.

In the winter of 1781 Mozart was in Munich, busy on the final stages of *Idomeneo*. Among the many musicians he met was Friedrich Ramm, an outstanding oboist, for whom he wrote a quartet, K. 370, which enjoys a deservedly high place in his chamber music. Ramm was no mere virtuoso: a contemporary account says that he played with exceptional depth of feeling and variety of tone. Mozart, taking full account of Ramm's powers, naturally gave the oboe all possible prominence, but he also contrived to make the string parts a good deal more expressive than they are in the flute quartets. The range of feeling too goes deeper. The *adagio*, a mere thirty-seven bars, in D minor, can stand comparison with any of Mozart's slow movements in this key, and plumbs depths which the B minor elegy in K. 285, for all its beauty, leaves untouched. The sparkling gaiety of the rondo is clouded only by the extraordinary passage of thirteen bars in which the oboe plays in 4/4 time against the continuing 6/8 lilt of the strings, with a rather eerie effect.

The last of these six 'solo' chamber works is the Quintet for horn and strings, K. 407, in E flat, which Mozart wrote in Vienna, probably towards the end of 1782. Like the four concertos for horn, this quintet was intended for Ignaz Leutgeb, a remarkable virtuoso who left the court orchestra at Salzburg to settle in Vienna, where he kept a cheesemonger's shop. He seems to have been a simple man and a loyal friend to Mozart, who indulged in affectionate verbal humour at his expense – humour which is reflected in the whimsical character of some of the music for the solo horn. It is not clear why in this quintet Mozart preferred to use the unusual pair of violas rather than the normal pair of violins; however, if he wanted to obtain a stronger balance in the middle strings to match the romantic sonority of the horn, he was wonderfully successful. For this is a lovely work, a concerto in miniature: its mood is a blend of cheerfulness and intimate feeling. The *andante* contains delightful passages of true chamber music, such as

EX. 4

where the discourse is based on one of Mozart's clichés, a phrase of four notes descending from a dotted quaver expanded from the opening theme, with an imaginative touch of contrary motion.

4. The First Three 'Haydn' Quartets

The early 1780s were a period of great crisis in Mozart's life, both emotionally and musically. When the Archbishop of Salzburg visited Vienna with his court in March 1781, Mozart's long-standing discontent boiled over and he was ignominiously dismissed in May. Deciding to stay in Vienna, he lived there for the rest of his life. He fell in love with Constanze Weber and married her in August 1782, sorely against his father's wishes. His determination to maintain his hard-won freedom seems to have released a spate of musical creativity. The success of *Die Entführung* began to spread his fame. He also became known as a brilliant pianist and as a composer of concertos: the circle of his friends grew rapidly, From his attendance at the concerts given by Baron Van Swieten. Director of the Imperial Library in Vienna, and a devotee of older music, Mozart widened his knowledge of J. S. Bach, and hence his understanding of counterpoint.

It is perhaps surprising that during these and many other activities Mozart could find much time for chamber music. That he did so was due initially to the renewed influence of Haydn, whom he met personally for the first time in December 1781. Shortly before this, Haydn had composed the six quartets Op. 33, which were published in 1782. Just as nine years before his quartets Op. 20 had made a deep impression on Mozart, so now the new works, usually called the 'Russian' quartets, inspired him to far greater heights.

When Mozart finished the first of his new quartets, on 31 December 1782, he probably had no plan for a set of six. Next April, however, he sent a prospective offer of such a set to Sieber in Paris. But nearly two years elapsed before he completed the sixth and entered it in his own thematic catalogue on 14 January 1785. This gap may, of course, be partly due to the fact that Mozart had become even more hectically busy as composer, performer and teacher. But there was another, deeper reason for it. When Artaria published the complete set in September 1785 it bore the justly famous dedication to Haydn, a highly personal and revealing document such as Mozart never wrote again:

'To my dear friend Haydn,

'A father who had resolved to send his children out into the great world took it to be his duty to confide them to the protection and guidance of a very celebrated Man, especially when the latter by good fortune was at the same time his best Friend. Here they are then, O great Man and my dearest Friend, these six children of mine. They are, it is true, the fruit of long and laborious endeavour, yet the hope inspired in me by several Friends that it may be at least partly compensated encourages me, and I flatter myself that this offspring will serve to afford me some solace one day. You yourself, dearest friend, told me of your satisfaction with them during your last Visit to this Capital. It is this indulgence above all which urges me to commend them to you and encourages me to hope that they will not seem to you altogether unworthy of your favour. May it therefore please you to receive them kindly and to be their Father, Guide and Friend! From this moment I resign to you all my rights in them, begging you however to look indulgently upon the defects which the partiality of a Father's eye may have concealed from me, and in spite of them to continue in your generous Friendship for him who so greatly values it, in expectation of which I am, with all my Heart, my dearest Friend, your most Sincere Friend

W. A. Mozart.'

'The fruit of long and laborious endeavour' – here is the key. Mozart had found it very much harder to absorb the lessons of Haydn's quartets Op. 33 than he had those of Op. 20 nine years before, simply because their achievement was so much greater.

When Haydn circulated his potential subscribers to Op. 33, he stated that these quartets were composed 'in an entirely new and special style'. These words may have been intended to attract curiosity: they are also musically significant. For he too had surmounted a crisis in his musical development, of which the essence lay at this time in the string quartet rather than in the symphony. He had mastered his art so completely that he was able to give all four instruments an equal share of the musical discourse, in any movement where he chose to do so. (The exceptions are usually in the slow movements, where the first violin may predominate.) Moreover, the so-called 'working-out' is not confined to the development section. He takes any portion of a theme, any scrap of melody, any rhythmical phrase and extracts every ounce of meaning so that the whole structure is both tautened and expanded. This innovation was the challenge Mozart had to face, and this is what lay behind the dedication.

These six quartets were composed in two groups, separated by a gap of about sixteen months. In various ways, they all cost Mozart much pains. The autographs bear this out, for they contain numerous corrections and erasures and some beginnings which Mozart rejected and cancelled. But the result was some flawless chamber music. Because Mozart had now learned to think, as it were, in four parts at will, instead of in terms of harmonized melody, this music has a spontaneous freshness and fluency of technique which is a never-ending source of wonder and delight to the listener.

The opening of the first quartet, K. 387, in G, embodies all these qualities. While the first subject is given to the first violin, the other three instruments converse, as it were, among themselves. The wide span of this flowing melody was certainly shaped as a contrast to the second subject, which is much more compact and has a rhythmical edge to it. The minuet is one of the most remarkable Mozart ever wrote. It departs completely from the formal rhythm: the rising chromatic scale, each note marked alternately *f* and *p*, is played on the first violin alone, and then in contrary motion on the cello, accompanied by the upper strings. The chromatic quality persists, though with progressively less pointed contrast, throughout the minuet. The trio, in G minor, is of much closer tissue. The effect of the first four bars, played in ferocious unison, is arresting. For the *andante*, Mozart moves to the calm of C major, and pours forth a stream of rapt, contemplative music, rich in gruppetti, soaring fioriture and beautifully calculated climaxes. It is a remarkable example of the sustained, exalted feeling expressed with wonderful harmonic resource, yet without a single melodic phrase that is at all memorable in itself. The finale, *molto allegro*, is cast in an extraordinary mould of polyphony and homophony blended into a movement of joyous release. The fugal exposition of the five-note semibreve subject (akin to that which begins the finale of the *Jupiter* Symphony) breaks off to admit a lilting dance tune, which is ultimately developed in counterpoint. The second subject proper is likewise treated contrapuntally, as is also a little six-note chromatic figure, which seems to echo that in the minuet. The short coda repeats this figure, and ends with a stretto of the opening semibreves.

Delightful as it seems to us today, we should not forget that Mozart's brilliant fertility of invention worried his contemporaries. Dittersdorf wrote: 'He leaves his hearer out of breath, for hardly has he grasped one beautiful thought than another of greater fascination dispels the first, and this goes on throughout, so that in the end it is impossible to retain any one of these beautiful melodies.' But it was not only a matter of elusive swiftness. The Vienna correspondent of the *Magazin der Musik* wrote thus of these very quartets in 1787:

'It is a pity that he aims too high in his artful and truly beautiful compositions, in order to become a new creator, whereby it must be said that feeling and heart profit little; his new Quartets for 2 violins, viola and bass, which he has dedicated to Haydn, may well be called too highly seasoned – and whose palate can endure this for long?'

Mozart's contemporaries were exercised by what they felt to be his continual straining after novelty, which obscured the 'feeling' (*Empfindung*). But in some of his music they must have found the 'feeling' disturbing.

Of few works is this truer than of the D minor quartet, K. 421, which dates from the summer of 1783. It moves in a different world from that of K. 173. According to a reliable tradition, it was composed during the birth of Constanze's first child, which took place on 17 June. But Mozart's natural anxiety can hardly be said to be related to the passionate melancholy which pervades most of the work. It is noticeable that in the opening bars of the first movement he does not write in four parts, but prefers a harmonic interest in the lower strings, as if to throw into sharper relief the angular melody on the first violin. But he uses his mastery of part-writing to the full in the development, particularly in the free use of a broken triplet figure bandied about by all four instruments, in the dozen bars or so which precede the recapitulation.

Throughout the *andante* (in F major, in 6/8) there is prominent a rising semiquaver figure, based on the spread notes of the common chord first heard in the third bar and interwoven with the rhythm of a broken quaver phrase which seems to create suspense by its indecisive hovering. This spread chord undergoes many slight changes of shape, and is one of the central threads in the restlessly shifting pattern which seems to express intense longing right up to the closing bars where the rising chord swells up and dies away. The tonal scheme is beautifully balanced throughout: there is one lovely passage where the key shifts from F minor to A flat major with almost Schubertian grace. At one point, in bars 47 and 48, Mozart uses three-note chords in first and second violin –

a very rare thing in these quartets, except to end a movement – to heighten the tension.

The mood and key of the first movement return in the minuet, and with it another marvel of four-part writing. At the heart of these thirty-eight bars lies the insistent dotted rhythm of the opening of the ten-bar melody which sets the instruments against each other, mostly in pairs, with masterly use of chromatic harmony. The trio, in D major, is like none other that Mozart ever wrote. It is marked 'sempre *p*'. The first violin plays the leaping, dotted melody over the other three strings pizzicato, but in the last eight bars is joined by the viola, playing arco over the continued pizzicato of cello and second violin. Despite the major key, the effect is eerie. For the finale Mozart returns to 6/8 (it is most unusual to find him writing two movements of the same quartet in this tempo), and composes a set of four variations on a siciliano-like theme (which bears some resemblance to that of Haydn's Op. 33, no. 5). The tempo cost Mozart some trouble. He wrote first *allegretto*, then deleted it in favour of *andante*, but finally preferred *allegretto ma non troppo*. Each variation is a contrast in mood and emphasis. In the first, the first violin plays florid elaborations of the melody. In the second, the two violins play mostly in violent cross-rhythms, over the smooth triplets of the viola, which is given unusual melodic prominence throughout most of the third variation. The fourth, moving smoothly in D major, introduces a gleam of untroubled light, with some eloquent passage work shared by viola and cello, before the D minor theme, now *più allegro*, recurs in an extended version as a coda. The repeated semi-quavers on the top A in the second and third bars return as triplets. When played insistently first an octave higher and then echoed by all the lower strings in succession, they heighten the expression of intense despair which is all the more poignant within the austere framework imposed by the variation form.

The third quartet, K. 428, in E flat, was probably finished within a few weeks of K. 421, and before the end of July 1783 at the latest. Like most of Mozart's other important works in this key, it has an inner warmth and serenity which here contrasts strongly with the turbulence of K. 421. This mood seems to be established by the rising octave of the first subject, which, unusually, the four instruments state in unison. But the style of dialogue quickly super-

venes, in a rapid interchange of little phrases on the violins. The
second subject is given to the first violin, and is restated at once
by the viola. The brief restatement of the first subject is in canon,
by way of variety, the violins being matched against the viola and
cello. The development is based on repetitions of the gruppetto
figure which opened the second subject and linked by a surge of
arpeggios in triplets which pass from one instrument to another
with arresting modulations. Characteristically, Mozart gives the last
appearance of the second subject to the second violin.

The *andante con moto* is in A flat and 6/8 time. Again, though the
movement is in sonata form, there is little melody which lingers in
the memory. The ninety-six bars are a richly harmonized, dream-
like meditation, a quiet, but restless inner searching heightened by
the use of chromatic syncopation. (In all Mozart's chamber music,
only the *adagio* of the great String Trio of 1788 offers any comparison.) A few bars will give some idea of this extraordinary
music:

EX. 5

Andante con moto

The resemblance between this passage and the opening of Wag-
ner's *Tristan* has rightly been pointed out in textbooks. The minuet
and trio bring the listener back to the world of everyday things,
and are not especially notable except perhaps for the very effective
succession of shifting cello pedal points in the trio, above which
the quavers move evenly from one voice to another. The finale, in
rondo form, is a light, airy fabric almost without shadows, but with
carefully balanced, symmetrical melodies. The most important
subsidiary theme, at bar 60, bears a close, perhaps subconscious,
resemblance to the second subject of the first movement.

5. Bach Arrangements; The String Duos

At this point, since Mozart wrote no more string quartets for over fifteen months, we can conveniently consider two excursions which he made into other forms of chamber music, roughly during the time covered by the first three 'Haydn' quartets. As already mentioned, it was in the spring of 1782 that Mozart began regularly to attend the Sunday morning concert organized by Baron Van Swieten at which, he wrote to his father, 'nothing is played but Handel and Bach', and went on: 'I am now collecting the fugues of Bach not only of Sebastian, but also of Emanuel and Friedemann.' For these concerts Mozart arranged as string trios (K. 404a) a number of pieces by J. S. Bach (three fugues from the '48', the *adagio* from the third Organ Sonata, the *largo* from the second, one fugue from the *Art of Fugue*) and the eighth of the fugues which Wilhelm Friedemann dedicated to Princess Amalie. For the last of these pieces and for the three fugues from the '48' Mozart wrote slow introductions, three in minor keys (F, G and D) and one in F major. As essays in string writing, these *adagios* are by no means unimpressive: it is interesting that three out of the four fugues which Mozart selected are in minor keys. Probably about the same time time he arranged six four-part fugues from Book II of the '48' for string quartet (K. 405).

In the summer of 1783 Mozart left Vienna and took his wife on a short visit to his father in Salzburg and it was here that he wrote the two duos for violin and viola (K. 423, in G, and K. 424, in B flat). There is a story that the Archbishop of Salzburg had commissioned Michael Haydn, the younger brother of Joseph and an old friend of Mozart's, to compose six such duos and that Haydn had only finished four when he was taken ill. The Archbishop is said to have withheld his pay as an incentive for him to recover and write the other two. When Mozart visited Haydn and heard of his plight, he went away, composed the two duos, and gave them to Haydn to pass with the others to the Archbishop under his own name. Four duets by Haydn are extant, but they are such mediocre works that one can only assume the Archbishop, being an indifferent judge of style, failed to notice how much superior to the rest the last two were. At any rate, Mozart clearly enjoyed helping Haydn, for these are both warm-hearted, lovely works and cast in the same mould as the great quartets, albeit on a smaller scale.

Each duo is in three movements only, and in each Mozart contrives to give the viola as much melodic prominence as consideration for tonal balance allows. Even when he assigns it an accompanying role, it is rarely dull. In passages where he resorts to judicious use of double-stopping, it is hard to realize that only two instruments are playing, for instance in these bars from the first movement of K. 423:

EX. 6

Later in the same movement there is a pleasing passage of canonic writing, which perhaps reflects the older use of duos as pieces for the display of erudition, just as some brilliant figuration is a relic of the virtuosity peculiar to this archaic form. Both the slow movements are serious and rich in invention. Perhaps the one movement which enshrines the finest characteristics of the two works – freshness, humour, latent dignity and technical skill – is the concluding theme and variations of K. 424. Its quality suggests that Mozart was composing for a double pleasure, to help a friend and to match his skill against the limitations of an unfamiliar medium.

6. The Last Three 'Haydn' Quartets

In 1784 Mozart composed mostly instrumental music – three sets of orchestral dances; five concertos for piano; the Quintet for piano and wind; sonatas for piano duet, piano solo, piano and violin; two sets of piano variations. Even during this activity, he was able to meet Haydn more often, and so may well have been inspired to compose another string quartet, which he completed on 9 November. This was the B flat Quartet, K. 458, now usually named *The Hunt*, from the 6/8 hunting-call style of its opening bars, to distinguish it from the later work, K. 589, in the same key.

B flat was for Mozart nearly always the key for the expression of happy, affectionate emotion and K. 458 is no exception. Here he keeps to the tonic in all the movements except the *adagio* (in E flat), but there is no feeling of monotony, because of the verve and variety of the rhythmical treatment. The mellifluous flow of the exposition, another lovely example of four-part thinking, gives way in bar 42 to a vigorous phrase, little more than a shake, which becomes the core of the second subject. It is tossed about from one instrument to another, as in a game of musical shuttlecock, and dominates the scene for thirty bars. After the double-bar, Mozart begins the development with a flowing tune in F, which lasts only sixteen bars before the game of shuttlecock returns, with many entrancing shifts of key, and goes on up to the recapitulation. Throughout the movement Mozart diversifies the 6/8 tempo as much as possible by displaced accents and cross-rhythms.

In the minuet and trio there is little of especial note, except that in half a dozen or so bars of each the limpid flow of this urbane music is disturbed by strong sforzandos as if to remind the hearer of hidden depths. Throughout all but ten bars of the trio, the second violin and the viola play together staccato, throwing into higher relief the smooth line of the first violin. The slow movement, in E flat, is an *adagio*, the only one so marked in all these six quartets. It is music of a quiet grandeur, all the more moving, perhaps, for its appearance in such generally gay surroundings. The melodic line is florid, but never over-decorated, and there is a wealth of rhythmical subtlety. Particularly striking are the two passages in the development where the first violin and the cello echo the sinuous tune antiphonally. By the simple use of evenly repeated semiquavers mounting into broken demisemiquavers, Mozart evokes a mood of quivering intensity which can better be felt than described in words. The whole movement enshrines the spirit of rapturous communication which is the essence of his chamber music. The buoyant finale returns to the opening mood and is in sonata form, with three well-defined subjects. As a whole, this movement is nearer to Haydn in style and spirit than any other in these quartets. Mozart contrives the grouping and contrasts of the four instruments with consummate artistry, and avoids any monotony from the rather square rhythms of the opening tune by diversifying the outline of the others (both in F), the second with wisps of rising semiquavers, and the third with delicate triplet figures.

Since Mozart entered the last two 'Haydn' quartets, K. 464, in A, and K. 465, in C, in his thematic catalogue respectively on 10 and 14 January 1785 they were clearly conceived as a close, distinctive pair, similar to the first two great String Quintets (p. 54). Moreover, as these two are separated from the *Hunt* by barely two months, the three works can also reasonably be regarded as a group. Hardly anywhere else in all Mozart's chamber music is there such an extraordinary antithesis between the remote, almost austere quality of K. 464 and the general ebullience of the *Hunt* on the one hand, and the confident power of K. 465 on the other. Although it has never been, and probably will not become, as popular as the other five, K. 464 has distinctive merits which should ensure it far more frequent performances than it receives. For a work of this period in a major key it has an unusually strong chromatic flavour. Study of its thematic content reveals an underlying unity which, whether consciously devised or not, is again unusual at this time. In this work, Mozart brings his art of the quartet as musical conversation to a new level of refinement. But the elusive detachment of the music as a whole seems to invest much of this conversation with the quality of understatement. It is some indication of its reticence that both the first and last movements are quite devoid of semiquavers, in place of which there serve, in the former, the brief triplets rounding off the second subject.

The opening of the first movement is characteristic of Mozart's love of symmetry and contrast. The first violin states the tune, with the other instruments in harmony for its first two and last four notes: this is repeated one note higher. Then all four in unison play an answering phrase twice, again repeated a degree higher than the first. The skill with which the latter phrase is used in the dialogue can be seen in these bars from the development:

EX. 7

A similar sequence of unison, one-note-higher repeat and a first violin passage marks the opening of the minuet. Its pattern consists mostly of subtle combinations of the two phrases from the first five bars with sustained tension of line and rhythm. For the trio, Mozart shifts from A major to the rarely used E major and loosens the fabric, with the melody first played over a descending scale on the cello and then beneath rippling triplets on the first violin.

The *andante*, in D major, is a set of six variations (the only slow movement of the six quartets in this form) on a tuneful, but rather angular theme which lends itself well to florid treatment. Each instrument has its fair share of prominence, notably in the fourth (minor) variation where the melody is virtually dissolved into the scamper of triplet semiquavers. The last variation is an extraordinary tour de force, in which the instruments meditate on the theme over a long rhythmical figure played mostly staccato, first for nineteen bars on the cello and then by its companions in succession and culminating in a variant with great skips on the first violin. The figure recurs on the cello to dominate the closing bars while the theme surges up and then dies away on the violins. The finale is constructed in sonata form, with supreme economy of what may here be described as 'thematic material' – for of melody, in the accepted sense, there is little. Instead, Mozart uses mere wisps of notes, the first four descending chromatically from the dominant, and rounded off by a twisted five-note phrase. These two phrases prove to be the mainsprings of the movement, which is one of Mozart's highest achievements in pure craftsmanship. By the time he reached the development, he seems to have felt that the lack of melodic contrast might prove rather monotonous, because he suddenly introduces an eight-bar tune of a type unparalleled in all his quartets. For the notes in all four parts are all semibreves or minims, and its hymn-like outline provides just the needed point of rest and change. It sounds even more effective when repeated by the first violin with a contrasting flow of quavers on the second. The recapitulation brings further refinements of part-writing, and it is characteristic of this elusive but engrossing movement that it dies away on the four opening notes, played pianissimo. It is the only quartet of Mozart's that ends with a whisper.

When the C major quartet was published in the autumn of 1785 it became the centre of a prolonged critical furore – not, of course, the whole work, but only the twenty-two bars of *adagio* introduction to the first movement. It was their harmonic audacities and false relations which disturbed the conventional ear. Some people believed Mozart had allowed the parts to be printed with many errors. But reference to the autograph shows that he wrote these bars with exceptional care and very few corrections, and that the parts of the first edition (of which he supervised the production) correspond to it exactly. When the matter was referred to Haydn, he is reputed to have remarked wisely that if Mozart wrote it so, he must have had his reasons for doing it. What were these reasons?

It seems most unlikely that Mozart intended deliberately to shock contemporary opinion. He surely wrote as he did to satisfy a twofold artistic need. These six quartets mark one of the great

peaks of his development. Fortified by his hard-won mastery of
the balance of form, style and feeling, he was driven on by his restless – almost demonic – urge to experiment and to search for new
means of expression. The general trend of these quartets shows
this clearly. He must have wanted the C major quartet to serve as
their climax. These introductory bars grip the hearer in an emotional vice. They create a mood of uncertainty and suspense, and
build up such tension that the release, when it comes, is cathartic.
Mozart had already used this device in the moving but rather art-
less *adagio* introducing K. 171. In K. 465 purpose and effect are on
a vastly higher plane. He was to use it again later in the *Prague*
Symphony and the D major String Quintet, for instance, and in a
number of the magnificent concert arias.

If there is one section of the *allegro* where Mozart's genius is seen
at its best, it is in the passage of almost fifty bars after the double-
bar. Here he takes the first part of the opening melody and develops it with a sustained wealth of modulation, rhythmical extension
and imitation. The whole movement is a triumph of imaginative
craftsmanship, linked to unflagging energy which is perfectly
controlled so that it enhances the essence of the quartet as a four-
part discourse. The *andante* is perhaps the most powerful slow
movement of all the six: the impact of its throbbing, almost ecstatic
intensity is something which cannot be diminished but is, rather,
strengthened by repeated hearings. The opening theme is, for
once, a lovely and memorable melody, in contrast to the more
conventional second subject. But, again, it is Mozart's treatment of
his material which is so fascinating, for the interest lies as much in a
subsidiary figure of four notes (*x*)

EX. 8

as in the main subjects. This pervasive figure is heard nearly seventy times in the course of these 114 bars, mostly in a rapturous overlapping dialogue between cello and first violin. It recurs on the second violin and cello as part of the ineffably lovely coda. One can also point to such purely musical devices as the crossing of the parts in the growth of the second subject, or to the way its outline mounts slowly through a span of over two octaves. But, even recognizing such technical felicities, it is, in the last resort, the mystery of Mozart's genius which seems to make time stand still, and transmutes sound into a deeply satisfying communication of spiritual values.

The minuet is an assertive piece with a distinctly chromatic flavour. The compact, sinuous melody passes smoothly among the instruments, singly or in pairs, in sharp contrast to the unison which answers it. For the trio, in C minor, Mozart devised a yearning tune, which rises and falls through wide melodic intervals, over a quiet, regular accompaniment on the second violin and viola, leaving only a discreet harmonic role to the cello. In the final *allegro molto* he strikes a mood which is happy without being ebullient, confident without being over-serious. The principal momentum comes from the quaver rhythm

EX. 9

of the opening theme, especially the notes marked *x*. They recur frequently as part of other melodies and serve to generate and control the immense vitality of the whole, with its wealth of invention, seen for instance in the handling of the third subject which is announced in an unprepared E flat, and reappears, just before the coda, first in A flat and then canonically treated in D flat. The entire finale sparkles with contrapuntal resource and swift, daring modulations of the kind which Mozart's contemporaries found so bewildering.

The reader may feel that the foregoing discussion of the 'Haydn' quartets has run to undue length in proportion to the space available for Mozart's whole output of chamber music. But it is indisputable that whatever he achieved in other forms, these six works enshrine the acme of his genius within their own range. Their variety makes them a treasure of inexhaustible delight. For most people, they begin to yield their secrets only after many hearings and long study of the scores. However limited their appeal in Mozart's own day, there was one person, Haydn, who divined their quality at the very time of their creation, and indeed heard what was certainly a very early performance of the first three quartets, and probably one of the earliest of the last three.

We owe our knowledge of this to some letters which Leopold Mozart wrote to his daughter. On 22 January 1785 he recounted news received from Wolfgang in Vienna and said: 'He adds that last Saturday [i.e. 15 January] he performed his six quartets for Haydn and other good friends.' Because K. 464 and K. 465 had only been finished on 10 and 14 January, this seems to refer to the first three quartets only. This point is established by a second letter, written on 16 February, by which time Leopold had gone to stay with his son in Vienna:

'On Saturday evening Herr Joseph Haydn and the two Barons Tinti came to see us and the new quartets were performed, or rather, the three new ones which Wolfgang has added to the other three which we have already. The new ones are somewhat easier but at the same time excellent compositions.'

(By 'easier', Leopold means that any trace of learned effort audible in K. 387, 421, 428 had quite gone.) He went on:

'Haydn said to me: "Before God and as an honest man I tell you that your son is the greatest composer known to me either in person or by name. He has taste and, what is more, the most profound knowledge of composition." '

This is surely one of the most generous and perceptive tributes ever paid by one great composer to another.

7. *Miscellaneous Chamber Music, mostly with Piano, 1778-88*

At this point we may digress from the sequence of the music for strings alone to consider a variety of other works, of which all save two have an important feature in common: the prominence of a piano. The best were written between the spring of 1784 and the autumn of 1788, the time when Mozart's fame as a composer and performer of concertos was at its height. In the thirteen superb concertos which bore public testimony to his brilliance, the role of the piano combined much of the bravura given to a great singer in an aria of *Figaro* or *Don Giovanni* with the thematic assertiveness inherent in the rivalry between solo and orchestra. Naturally, though to a varying degree, the influence of Mozart's concerto style is seen in most of his contemporaneous chamber works with piano. Here, however, the keyboard is a prominent partner rather than an antagonist. The silvery, yet penetrating tone of the fortepiano ensured that even in the tuttis no other instrument had to struggle to make itself heard. The piano could therefore assert much of its traditional thematic primacy and yet also, as *primus inter pares*, preserve the balance of the musical structure.

The four principal works are the Quintet for piano and wind, the two Quartets for piano and strings, and the Trio for piano, clarinet and viola. (The last of these, because of its distinctive tone-colour, can better be introduced here than with the other piano trios with which it is usually published.) The Quintet for piano, oboe, clarinet, horn and bassoon, K. 452, in E flat, was completed on 30 March 1784, and received its first performance two days later, at one of the Lent concerts given at the Imperial and Royal National Court Theatre in Vienna. Mozart himself played the piano part: the names of the other players are unrecorded. Writing to his father on 10 April, he said he thought it was the best work he had written in his life. This was a high claim for the composer to make. But notwithstanding all the fine works his rapidly maturing genius had produced from 1778 onwards, Mozart was probably right, at that time. For this Quintet is an indisputable masterpiece. In it Mozart strikes a fine compromise between display and feeling: he does not sacrifice depth to brilliance.

The proportions of the movements are unusual. The first, including a *largo* introduction of twenty bars, is only 122 bars in all. The *larghetto* is actually two bars longer, and the rondo runs to 238. Unusually, Mozart concentrated all the weight in the first two movements. The introduction is a thing of rare warmth and dignity, in which he slowly unfolds the rich patterns of sonority at his command. Here, as throughout, after giving each player due prominence, he builds up to a fine climax with the wind playing tutti above a sequence of sustained trills on the piano. The whole *allegro* is full of the happiest invention and variety. Mozart blends the instruments in pairs, in threes or fours so ingeniously that what he omits makes the remainder sound all the more fresh and attractive. In the *larghetto* in B flat he strikes a more majestic vein than is usual for this key. Some striking passages of broken chords and arpeggios for the piano provide an iridescent backcloth for the grouping and regrouping of the wind in gentle rivalry. The finale, *allegretto*, may sometimes seem to veer towards the concertante style, but the equality of the five partners always reasserts itself. The horn, for instance, playing in close imitation of the oboe, shares the statement of the second subject, in C minor. Perhaps the most delightful part of the rondo is the long enchanting cadenza which, written for all five players, miraculously remains within the bounds of chamber music.

The two Piano Quartets have a curious history. Nissen says that the earlier, in G minor, K. 478 (completed 16 October 1785) was the first of three commissioned by the publisher Franz Anton Hoffmeister (also a prolific minor composer), who issued a number of Mozart's chamber and keyboard works. When the public found it too difficult, Mozart did not hold him to the contract. Nissen further says that Hoffmeister let Mozart keep the advance payment, stipulating only that he should not compose the remaining quartets. But on 3 June 1786 Mozart did complete one more, the E flat, K. 493, and it was published by Artaria in 1787. Whatever the truth of this story, the facts and the high quality of the music show that in this medium, too, Mozart faced and overcame a challenge. He virtually created the piano quartet, since earlier eighteenth-century works for keyboard and three strings were miniature concertos. In these Mozart quartets the difficult keyboard part proclaims their clear affinity with his great concertos, but the intimacy and balance are of a more private world.

In both quartets, Mozart treats the cello with discretion, giving it mostly a supporting role either in conjunction with the other strings or else amplifying the harmony or rhythm of the keyboard bass. All the more effective is its individual voice, as in the development section of the finale of K. 493 where it echoes the piano, or the florid demisemiquavers given to it in the *andante* of K. 478. Mozart's part-writing is masterly, as can be seen in this example from the first movement of K. 478:

EX. 10

This emphatic statement of the main subject in octaves typifies the imperious, passionate mood of this quartet, which may well have sounded strange to the Viennese public. The lyrical beauty of the *andante* in B flat is founded on some wonderfully rich harmony which never cloys, but throws into sharper relief the shift to G major for the confident vigour of the rondo, where Mozart cleverly exploits the alternation of keyboard and strings. The first movement of K. 493 is notable for the taste and skill with which the pivotal opening of the second subject

EX. II

Allegro

is repeated – thirty-seven times in all – as the unifying source of much of the thematic interest. For the *larghetto*, Mozart again uses A flat, and as in K. 428 creates music of spiritual intensity, tinged with a chromatic warmth which glows through all the parts. It would seem that the eight opening bars of the *allegretto* (given to the piano alone) cost Mozart some pains, for there exist two earlier attempts which evolve into the smoothly accented rhythmical curve that finally satisfied him. Throughout, the craftsmanship and the poetic treatment of the melodies let the hearer revel in the delight of the music. How fresh, for instance, in the eight bars leading to the first recapitulation, is the dialogue between the violin and the treble of the piano, pointed by acciaccature which seem to make the bright notes sparkle over the smooth bass of the piano fortified by the viola! It sounds so inevitably right.

Only two months later, on 5 August 1786, Mozart completed another original masterpiece, the Trio in E flat, K. 498, for piano, clarinet and viola. He wrote it for his piano pupil Franziska von Jacquin, the sister of his close friend the Baron Gottfried, for whose musical circle (probably including the clarinettist Anton Stadler) Mozart wrote other delightful pieces. One would like to think that he may have played the highly rewarding viola part himself. Its warm, veiled tone-colour blends perfectly with the sensuous range and depth of the clarinet. For all its mellifluousness, this Trio is a work of astonishing power, the secret of which lies partly in the equality of partnership between the three instruments. In the 129 bars comprising the taut first movement (a virtually monothematic *andante*), the principal melody, based on the common chord and a simple gruppetto, is heard forty-one times in all, fifteen times on the clarinet and seven on the viola. The latter has an even more generous share of the triplets which scurry throughout the sombre minuet, while in the song-like finale the distribution of melodic interest is fairly maintained throughout, and enriched and strengthened with unobtrusive counterpoint.

There is a slightly dubious tradition that Mozart wrote the Clarinet Trio while playing skittles (it is called in German the *Kegelstatt* Trio). This pastime was however unquestionably associated with the twelve Duets for two horns, K. 487, which he completed on 27 July 1786, for he stated on the autograph that they were composed 'untern Kegelscheiben'. Though most of the movements do not exceed thirty bars, these are delightful little pieces, full of happy melodic and technical invention. Were they perhaps intended for Leutgeb and another unknown horn-player among the friends of Mozart and Jacquin? Another chamber work composed for the Jacquin circle, probably in December 1787, is the Quartet for flute and strings, in A, K. 298. Formerly thought to have been one of the group of such works written in Paris during the winter 1777 to 1778, its later date has now been accepted from the style of Mozart's handwriting and from the fact that the autograph once belonged to Baron von Jacquin. This is a melodious piece, transparent in style and with a finale notable for the attractive way in which the main tune is freely bandied about by the strings when the flute is silent.

It was about this time that Mozart finished the first two of the five Trios for piano, violin and cello composed in his maturity. (An early work in B flat, K. 254, of 1776, and an assortment of unfinished movements making the Trio in D minor, K. 442, August 1783, are of little moment.) The first two, K. 496, in G, and K. 502, in B flat, were completed respectively on 8 July and 18 November 1786. The last three all date from 1788, the E major, K. 542, completed on 22 June, the C major, K. 548, on 14 July, and the second G major, K. 564, on 22 October. The medium was a popular one in Vienna, and, as none of the five bears any dedication, it seems likely that Mozart wrote them to make money. But they may also originally have been intended for private enjoyment.

Even more than in the Piano Quartets, the cello is usually unobtrusive, and takes a slender part in the dialogue, either strengthening the bass or playing in harmony or unison with the violin. Its occasional prominence is therefore all the more effective, as in two similar passages in the slow movement of K. 496 and the first movement of K. 542 where it plays in close imitation of the violin. The last page or so of the finale of K. 502 shows the two strings combining in free rivalry with the piano.

Within such limitations, and accepting the superior role of the violin, the best of these trios rank high among Mozart's chamber masterpieces. The earlier in G, K. 496, has all the bold, assertive vigour and sweeping melodies common to earlier chamber works in this key, such as K. 387 and K. 423. The first movement sparkles with arresting modulations and verges on the dramatic in the explosive mood of the development. The variations comprising the slow movement are in Mozart's happiest vein of inventive contrast. Good though the best of K. 496 is, it is far exceeded by K. 502 and K. 542. The former has much of the charm and technical brilliance of the piano concertos in this key, K. 450 and K. 456. For the latter, in a key which Mozart seldom used, no praise can be too high. Its texture is transparent and the prevailing mood seems to be one of vernal happiness. But the radiance is shot through with a sadness which is intensified by almost Schubertian modulations to remote keys. The same ambiguity pervades the *andante grazioso*, a miracle of haunting simplicity, which again anticipates Schubert. Nor does the inspired craftsmanship of the glittering finale, with its brilliant passage-work in triplets for the violin, wholly dispel he mood of wistfulness.

The last two trios, K. 548 and K. 564, mark a sad falling off from the high standard of their predecessors. For all their outward gaiety and verve, they lack tautness of construction and fresh invention; the intimacy, too, is gone. This falling-off may reflect the intermittent exhaustion and fluctuating creative power that overtook Mozart even during the period of his last three symphonies.

After his juvenile violin sonatas of 1766, Mozart wrote no more until 1778. During the next ten years, he composed just over a score of sonatas (three of which he left unfinished) and two sets of variations. Although except in the three masterpieces of his maturity the role of the violin is often secondary, these works contain some strikingly original music. The fact that Mozart, or his various publishers, regularly described the violin as an accompanying instrument, should not prejudice one's judgement. For this was how composers, players and audiences continued to regard the violin in the later eighteenth century. In fact, sixteen years after Mozart wrote his last sonata, Beethoven's Sonatas Op. 30 (1803) were described on the title page of the first edition as 'pour le piano-forte avec l'accompagnement d'un violon', and two years later his *Kreutzer* Sonata was similarly described, with the added qualification that it was 'scritto in uno stilo molto concertante'.

It is, indeed, the concertante treatment of the violin part (although naturally less adventurous than Beethoven's) that colours the interest of the seven sonatas which Mozart wrote in the first half of 1778. Six of them (K. 301–306) were later printed with a dedication to Maria Elisabeth, Electress of the Palatinate. From a letter written to his father, we know what induced Mozart to compose them. He said he had come across six violin sonatas by 'Schuster' (who was, probably, Joseph Schuster, Kapellmeister to the Court at Dresden), and intended to write six himself in the same style. Unfortunately, as no relevant works by Schuster can be traced, we do not know how much the style of Mozart's sonatas owes to him. But it is clear that he had still not forgotten the earlier influences of J. C. Bach and Schobert.

When the piano has the melody, the violin may play dull accompaniment figures, or simply lend harmonic or rhythmical support to the keyboard. But in nearly all the movements of these sonatas there are passages where the violin becomes an alternating partner and sometimes even more. Undoubtedly the most arresting work is K. 304, in E minor, for in most of its first movement Mozart treats the two instruments as a unit of great dramatic force, and much of the piano part hardly makes musical sense without the violin. The coda is of almost Beethovenian power. Equally bold are parts of the sonata in D (K. 306), especially the *andante*, which is practically an arioso for the violin.

The next five sonatas (K. 378, 379, 376, 377, 380, the first dating from early in 1779, the others written from April to June 1781) all show a considerable advance in the free, concertante treatment of the violin part. K. 377, in F, has a slow movement consisting of variations in D minor, comparable in their brooding intensity to those of the Serenade in D, K. 334, and to the finale of K. 421. Solo and keyboard interweave in perfect equality. Another very fine conception is the first movement of K. 379, in G, with its powerful introduction leading to an *allegro* in G minor throughout which the violin is, again, an equal partner in a passionate dialogue. Whereas in Mozart's other music of this time the influence of various composers can be traced, in these five sonatas he seems to have drawn on nothing except his own inspiration. This is even more true of the three finest sonatas, which, like some of his other chamber works with keyboard already mentioned, date from the time of the great piano concertos and were in some degree influenced by them.

Although Mozart entered the B flat Violin Sonata, K. 454, in his thematic catalogue on 21 April 1784, he did not complete it until some time later. He composed it for Regina Strinasacchi, a famous violinist from Mantua, whose playing he much admired, and with whom he gave the first performance at the Kärntnerthor Theatre in Vienna on 29 April. An interesting story was later told by the composer's widow. The Emperor Joseph, who was present, thought he could see, through his glass, that Mozart had no music before him. He had him summoned and requested him to bring the sonata. It was blank music paper divided into bars, Mozart having had no time to write out the piano part, which he thus played from memory, without rehearsal. This story is virtually borne out by the state of the autograph, in which the use of different inks, unusually erratic bar-lines and miscalculation of space, show that Mozart wrote the violin part first and squeezed the piano part in later. Like K. 502, this sonata has much of the warmth and inventive brilliance of the two piano concertos in the same key, K. 450 and K. 456. Perhaps the two most arresting parts of it are the short, but majestic introductory *largo*, and the almost rhapsodical slow movement, where the violin part blends intimacy with virtuosity.

By comparison, its successor, in E flat, K. 481, completed on 12 December 1784, seems a rather austere work and we do not know why Mozart wrote it: possibly it was to a commission from the publisher Hoffmeister. Throughout, the instruments share an animated partnership of restrained sonority. One of the most striking passages in the first movement is that where, over sighing broken chords on the piano, the violin plays a rising sequence of four notes nearly identical with those which open the finale of the *Jupiter* Symphony. The profound *adagio*, in A flat, is full of striking modulations, one of which, leading through D flat and C sharp minor to A major, evokes a mood of rare intensity. In the finale, consisting of six variations on a sinewy theme, Mozart veers strongly towards the concertante style, especially in the change to 6/8 time for the last variation, with something of the same effect that he achieved at the end of the Concerto in E flat, K. 449.

The third of these great sonatas is the A major, K. 526, which Mozart completed on 24 August 1787: whether for his own performance or for others, is not known. In this wonderful composition he brought to perfection the balance between display and feeling, moulded by a melodic fluency which has much in common with that of the A major Concerto, K. 488. Again, there is perfect equality between the two instruments, strengthened by much effortless use of counterpoint. It is no little testimony to the enduring freshness and power of the best of Mozart's violin sonatas that they are practically the only ones of their period still in regular concert performance today.

8. *Various Works for Strings, 1786–8*

Even during these hectic years in Vienna, when so many different kinds of music made heavy demands on Mozart's time and energy, he could not resist for long the attraction of composing chamber works for strings alone. Barely nineteen months after the six 'Haydn' quartets he wrote another, the D major, K. 499. Completed on 19 August 1786, it is usually known as the 'Hoffmeister' after the name of its publisher, to distinguish it from the later one in the same key. Possibly, like the first Piano Quartet, it was written at the publisher's suggestion. The isolated position of

K. 499 in the sequence of Mozart's quartets has some similarity to that of Beethoven's Op. 95.

It is a rather strange work, lacking perhaps the immediacy and touching qualities of the best of its predecessors but by no means inferior to them in artistry. Such elusive, ambiguous music repays prolonged study. Throughout the whole quartet, the four instruments are equal partners in a discourse in which the melodies and phrases flow freely from one voice to another. The gentle pace of the opening *allegretto* is diversified by the sharply contrasting rhythms of the several themes, of which the first consists of a simple chordal idea, stated in unison. The germ of this protean melody, restated sometimes in inversion or with many changes and fragmentations of outline, really dominates the movement. Some remarkable key sequences contribute to the mood of disquiet which pervades the music up to the double bar. At this point Mozart introduces an eight-note close-knit quaver figure which, played staccato, sounds like a ticking clock. Expanded by the instruments variously grouped in pairs, it serves as the background for a bold, sequential repetition of the opening theme, finely conceived with many shifts of key. The coda consists of the same juxtaposition, with the insistent quaver figure dying away to a pianissimo.

In the minuet Mozart combines a shapely tune with a remarkable quasi-independence of the parts and some nice touches of chromaticism in the middle ones. In the rather sombre trio, he moves into D minor, and writes throughout in triplets, with strong, sudden contrasts between forte and piano. The *adagio*, in G, is not perhaps among the most deeply felt of Mozart's slow movements, for it is rather reticent and suggests a mood of half-remembered grief. The sheer beauty of the sound is enhanced by the imaginative variety of the part-writing. The *allegro*, though in 2/4, is dominated by the vigorous triplet rhythms in which the first melody is stated. The frequent sudden pauses and broken phrases suggest affinity with some of Haydn's quartet finales, but the mood, again, is elusive. Is it one of wry humour, or one of veiled sadness, despite the major key? Even a secondary melody, first heard on the cello, consists of a triplet figure scurrying upwards. Whenever Mozart brings in a theme in duple time, he never lets it run for long without interruption by triplets, often given to the viola or cello. It is these triplets (surely derived from the idea in the trio), combined with the abrupt style, which makes this finale quite different from anything in the earlier quartets.

For nearly three years after K. 499 Mozart composed no more complete string quartets. During this time, however, he wrote two of the four string quintets, which will be discussed later, and completed two other masterpieces for strings: the C minor Adagio introductory to his quartet arrangement of the C minor fugue for two pianos, and the Trio in E flat. We do not know what induced him to write this Adagio, K. 546, completed on 26 June 1788, nor why he chose to link it with the magnificent fugue of 1783. (Is it just a coincidence that the two important works which Mozart chose to arrange for strings in the late 1780s – this fugue and the later of the two wind octets – are both in C minor?)

K. 546, a mere fifty-two bars, is one of the peaks in Mozart's treatment of the quartet. It equals, if indeed it does not surpass, the introduction to K. 465, as an example of the art of building up tension and suspense and then relaxing it without anticlimax. Here, as in the slow movement of Beethoven's Fourth Piano Concerto, the music is not so much a discourse as an altercation, in which outbursts of passionate protest are answered, as it were, by the firm statements of reason, which gain gradual acceptance. The jagged leaps of the opening phrase are answered by a gentle rocking figure in F minor which passes through all the voices. The opening recurs and rises chromatically to G minor. One can only surmise what Mozart's contemporaries may have thought of the grating suspensions and harsh modulations through which this pattern is repeated before the last piercing cry of the first violin dies away and the rocking rhythm wins the argument. In the closing bars, Mozart lets it flow through each instrument in turn, as the tonality passes from F minor to A minor and comes to rest in the illusory calm of G major, before the violence of the fugue erupts in C minor. Mozart's transcription of his own work is so masterly that the elaborate contrapuntal texture gains in clarity from the varied colour of the strings compared with the more limited dynamic of the keyboard. In the autograph of the quartet version Mozart wrote the words 'Violoncelli' and 'contrabasso' against the bass stave, which suggests he may have also had in mind performance by a string orchestra.

In the summer of 1788, he entered the saddest period of his

whole life. Oppressed by family cares, still without any regular income except the meagre salary from his official post and thus always short of money and in debt, it is hardly surprising that he became ill and that his creative energy began to decline to its lowest point. For six weeks after finishing the *Jupiter* Symphony on 10 August, he wrote no music except a dozen canons. But on 27 September he completed another masterpiece, the String Trio in E flat, K. 563, which proved, however, to be his last work of any significance for nearly nine months. We know from one of Mozart's letters that he wrote this Trio for Michael Puchberg, a wealthy merchant who was a fellow freemason and one of the most loyal friends of these last years, and for whom he had also composed K. 542. Puchberg responded with unfailing generosity to the many pathetic appeals for money which Mozart made to him from June 1788 to April 1791. As a skilled musician, he must have appreciated K. 563 as an early token of gratitude for loans which he probably knew Mozart could never repay.

Mozart entered the work in his catalogue as 'Ein Divertimento a 1 Violino, 1 Viola, e Violoncello: di sei Pezzi'. Here he reverted to a title which he had not used for eleven years, and to a medium which he otherwise used only in the preludes written for the Bach fugue arrangements of 1782. The choice of this difficult and unfamiliar medium suggests that here Mozart was challenging his own powers, as if to test and prove his self-confidence at a time of great trouble and renewed anxiety. This tribute to his friend, while deeply felt and serious, is serene and happy music, with no trace of despair. (One wonders, however, if the use of the archaizing title 'Divertimento' was a piece of deliberate irony.) For the hour, it seemed that Mozart could reaffirm his faith in humanity through his longest chamber work. Indeed, the extended plan – *allegro, adagio,* minuet, *andante* (theme and variations), minuet, *allegro* – suggests this. But such is his command of technique and sonority that length never becomes an end in itself; each movement is perfectly proportioned in relation to the whole. The result is a unique masterpiece fully equal to the best of the 'Haydn' Quartets.

Throughout, Mozart maintained a remarkable equality between the three voices. Whichever instrument (or pair of them) leads, the accompanying role is rarely conventional for long. The viola part is one of the most attractive he ever wrote, not surprisingly, perhaps, as he preferred to play this instrument, and is known to have taken part in three performances of the work. Every movement abounds in happy invention, of which a few instances must suffice. In the opening bars of the *adagio* the cello plays a simple arpeggio figure, which rises over little more than an octave. At its first repeat, on the violin in the dominant, it swells into new life and soars up, fortified with gruppetti, over a span of more than two octaves. The full impact of this simple figure is reserved for the end of the movement, where it completely dominates the last dozen bars or so, as it is repeated by each player in succession. Alpha has indeed become omega.

The variations rank among Mozart's very finest. One section flows into the next without a break, and the treatment of the long theme, which sounds as if it might have some affinity with folk-song, takes the form of meditative allusion rather than melismatic ornamentation. The third section has a remarkable passage where a vigorous dialogue between violin and viola alternates with violin and cello playing in canon. In the digression to B flat minor, Mozart revels in over thirty bars of triple counterpoint:

EX. 12

Reverting to the major, he lifts the music to a yet higher plane by an old but most effective device. The theme, reduced to skeletal outline, is given to the viola in the manner of an extended *cantus firmus*, accompanied by continuous demisemiquavers on the violin and semiquavers on the cello. So remote has the theme become from its original form that the partial restatement in the closing bars falls quite freshly on the ear.

At the opening of the rondo, Mozart indulges in the gentle humour of the unexpected. The placid, heart-easing melody flows on, cushioned on unbroken triplets on the viola for thirty-five bars (probably a record length in any of his works), with only sparse quavers on the cello. Then this pungent drum-like phrase

EX. 13

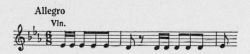

suddenly changes the whole picture. It becomes one of the main pivots in the tonal and formal plan to which it gives variety and strength. Its insistent, imitative repetition throughout the last twenty bars or so provides just the emphatic ending needed to fulfil the assertive character of the Divertimento. Truly Puchberg must have been delighted with this present of 'infinite riches in a little room'.

9. The Three 'Prussian' Quartets

In the early months of 1789 Mozart's plight continued to be as desperate as ever, with little prospect of improvement. Towards the end of March, his friend and pupil Prince Karl Lichnowsky offered to take him to Berlin and introduce him to Frederick William II, King of Prussia, an enthusiastic cellist and a pupil of Carlo Graziani and J. P. Duport. Mozart accepted, probably as much with relief at the prospect of temporary escape from Vienna as with hope of betterment. The most important result of this journey was the three so-called 'Prussian' quartets, which are mentioned in four of Mozart's letters, written to Puchberg. Each passage deserves quotation in its full context. On 12 July 1789 when Constanze was ill again, he wrote one of the most abject of all his begging letters:

'Instead of paying my debts I am asking for more money! ... at last I am beginning to feel inclined for work. ... I am composing six easy clavier sonatas for Princess Friederike and six quartets for the King.'

Early in May 1790 he wrote:

'I still feel very unwell. ... When I move out of these quarters I shall have to pay 275 gulden towards my new home. But I must have something to live on until I have arranged my concerts and until the quartets on which I am working have been sent to be engraved.'

And about a week later:

'Alas, I must still ask you to wait patiently for the sums I have been owing you for such a long time. If only you knew what grief and worry all this causes me. It has prevented me all this time from finishing my quartets. ... Next Saturday I intend to perform my quartets at home, and request the pleasure of your company and that of your wife.'

Lastly, on 12 June:

'For economy's sake I am staying at Baden and only come into town when it is absolutely necessary. I have now been obliged to give away my quartets (such a troublesome task) simply in order to have cash in hand to meet my present difficulties.'

After Mozart returned from Berlin to Vienna on 4 June 1789, he began the Quartet in D, K. 575, immediately and entered it in his catalogue in that month. (At this time, the entries give only the month, without the day.) Between this and the second Quartet, in B flat, K. 589, there is a gap of eleven months, due partly to the demands of *Così fan tutte*. K. 589 was completed in May 1790, and the F major, K. 590, in June. All three were published a few weeks after Mozart's death by Artaria, who advertised them as 'concertante quartets'. They bore no dedication to the King of Prussia, as they probably would have if Mozart had without delay composed the remaining three.

From this sequence of dates and from their relation to the letters quoted above, two important questions arise. Why did he fail to finish the intended set of six quartets, and why did he find the work of composing the first three so 'troublesome' ('mühsam')? The first is easier to answer. Before the journey to Berlin, and even more so after it, Mozart found consistent creative effort increasingly difficult. Friendship and gratitude could inspire the String Trio. The demands of an opera could rouse his genius from the depths of despair. But just as he simply could not compel himself to write more than one piano sonata for Princess Friederike, so he simply could not give his mind to more than half of the set of six quartets for Frederick William II. The task became impersonal and Mozart must have realized that even if completed it would have brought little more than temporary relief.

It is less easy to understand exactly what caused him to describe the task of composition as 'troublesome'. His use of a similar phrase in the dedication of the 'Haydn' Quartets – 'the fruit of long and laborious endeavour' – suggests that quartet-writing would always have taxed his powers even in the happiest circumstances. Still more taxing must it have been when he returned from his northern tour to face the harsh realities of worry and impoverishment in Vienna. He had to begin the quartets as soon as possible, and face the technical problem of giving prominence to the royal cello.

How far this in itself added to Mozart's anxieties, it is hard to say. But it seems certain that he lost his power of detachment and that self-doubt caused temporary failure of inspiration. There is no other possible explanation of the astonishing fact that, in order to start K. 575 and K. 589, he had recourse to the manuscripts of quartets begun in outline but for some reason discarded probably at least nine years earlier.[1] (The use of a discarded draft to stimulate flagging invention is not unknown with other composers, for instance with Handel.)

The influence of the royal cellist can be found throughout the

---

[1] As Einstein saw, the evidence is in the autographs, now in the British Museum. For the whole of K. 575 and the first six leaves of K. 589 Mozart used the rather coarse, greyish ten-stave paper on which he wrote most of his works up to the end of 1781–2 but to which thereafter he preferred a whitish-brown paper, more economically ruled with twelve staves. There is no other instance of Mozart using ten- and twelve-stave paper for a complete instrumental work, as for K. 589. These autographs also show two distinct styles of handwriting, which cannot be entirely explained by the idea that within eleven months or so he used quills of different thickness.

three quartets, in about a dozen passages, most markedly in K. 575. Such prominence contributes to the concertante effect mentioned in the title of the first edition. When the cello moves up into the alto register, sometimes even into the treble, the other strings assume an accompanying role, as in the *andante* of K. 575

EX. 14

or the *allegro* of K. 589 where the cello soars to top A. This shift in the normal balance was another reason for Mozart's description of the quartets as 'troublesome', borne out by the heavy corrections in the autographs. But in the process Mozart discovered a new beauty of elevated string tone. The texture becomes generally lighter, even when the royal bias is quite forgotten, for instance in the minuet of K. 590.

Comparison with the seven preceding quartets shows that structural and formal changes also took place. In only three of them did Mozart place the minuet third, but it stands here in all the 'Prussian' quartets. Similarly, in the first two of the great string quintets (1787) the minuet stands second, but third in the last two (1790, 1791). The earlier quartets were all notable for their highly organized thematic development: in most of them there was little difference in this respect between the first and fourth movements. But in the 'Prussian' quartets, Mozart paid less attention to thematic working, composed each first movement in a light, melodious style, and shifted most of the weight to the finale, with much contrapuntal elaboration, especially in the last two quartets. Compared, again, with those of the preceding quartets, many of the themes of the last three are of quite a different shape and the phrase-lengths tend to be longer, deliberately asymmetrical, with irregular stresses. In general, it would seem that here, partly from the challenge of the King's instrument, Mozart sought to redefine some of the values and principles he had established between 1783 and 1786.

Some characteristics of each of the three quartets deserve mention. In the first movement of K. 575 Mozart used the uncommon direction 'sotto voce' both at its opening and later. He also marks some passages 'dolce'. He repeated both these directions in the *andante*, thus emphasizing its affinity of mood, albeit in the unusual relationship of the dominant, A major. Neither in these movements nor in the minuet is the cello so prominent as in the trio or the finale. In the latter (a rondo) it announces the principal theme, which is clearly derived from that of the *allegro*, and has a powerful voice in such striking contrapuntal passages as this:

EX. 15

This melody and its derivatives dominate the rondo to such an extent that they are heard in nearly half of its 230 bars. Mozart alternates sections of polyphonic treatment with the pure melody supported by figuration of charming variety. Whatever may have been his mood when he began this quartet, its finale rises to serene happiness expressed in this main theme and the subsidiary one in A major.

The first movement of K. 589 is subdued, even reflective, and the melodic threads are loosely spun. The chief interest lies in the contrast between the neat, downward-curling opening melody and the two subsidiary tunes, each a lovely example of Mozart's *cantabile* style, and each announced by the cello, sometimes soaring high into the treble. Variety comes from the rather gawky triplet passages which either link or sometimes accompany the themes. In the *larghetto*, Mozart once more favoured the cello, writing what is virtually an arioso with florid scale-passages both for the soloist and the accompaniment. While the minuet is uneventful, the trio is most remarkable. It is the longest of any in the ten last quartets, for its sixty-six bars are approached only by the fifty-four of the trio in K. 387. The structure, too, is unparalleled. The incessant figuration, which underlies the rather square tune, sounds peculiar, even more so when transformed in the second section into leaping, angular phrases on the first violin. Even more striking is the short transition passage of fifteen bars after the double bar, where a repeated, almost angrily sighing figure jerks the tonality to D flat, and sinks back to the tonic after a long pause. In the compact finale, only 155 bars, Mozart reasserts the full equality of all four instruments, and treats the thematic material with extraordinary skill, by inversion, by imitation, and contrapuntally. All are so briefly used that the music has an Ariel-like, evanescent quality which belies its latent strength.

The first movement of K. 590, like that of its predecessors, is relatively uneventful. The distinctive opening theme is a long, sprawling affair, a statement and answer with delicately irregular stresses. One point of interest is the way in which Mozart uses the little five-note phrase from the end of the answer as the topic of brisk discussion, rather as in the first movement of K. 458. The melodic thread is spun lightly, thus making all the more effective the four bars of a powerful restatement of the opening theme in unison just before the subdued ending. The *andante* is a meditation on a simple rhythmical phrase which is heard in all but barely a dozen of the 123 bars. (Something of its shape and treatment are found in *Figaro* – Act 2, scene 9, *molto andante* – at the moment of suspense when Susanna emerges from the locked room, to the Count's confusion and the Countess's astonished relief.) Round and through its repetitions, which often overlap between one voice and another, Mozart weaves a continually shifting web of modulation and decorative patterns, while also giving prominence to the cello. The intensity of the slow movements of the 'Haydn' quartets has here given way to quiet contemplation.

While there is some similarity between the melody of the minuet and that of K. 589, the shape is quite different. So too is the unusual proportion of accompaniment given to the first violin. It is partly this, and partly the irregularity of the phrase-lengths (seven bars in the minuet, five in the trio) which give the whole movement a somewhat bizarre quality. The capricious element is again the *allegro*, where a continual torrent of semiquavers almost becomes a *perpetuum mobile*. Using a combination of rondo and sonata form, Mozart avoids monotony by breaking off on pedal points and pauses (as in K. 499) which create uneasy silences emphasized by unexpected shifts of key. One of the most electrifying occurs at the double bar, where a plunge into D flat follows a cadence on the dominant. Mozart whirls the movement to its climax through flurries of fugato, strongly displaced accents and a drone bass which combine with the tremendous élan of the music to make this one of the most irresistible and original finales in all the quartets. As in K. 589, all four instruments are equal partners; where the cello is prominent, its role is conceived in polyphonic terms and not as a possible gratification of royal vanity.

New beauty of string tone, some preference for thematic uniformity, a strong concentration of interest in the finales, and in them a brilliant, vigorous use of fugato – such are the salient features of the last three quartets. Although Mozart wrote no more, he developed these qualities in other works, notably in the last two of the four great string quintets. It was in them that he gradually combined and intensified the strength and rich variety of the 'Haydn' Quartets and the String Trio with the distinctive refinements of the 'Prussian' Quartets.

10. *The String Quintets*

Mozart's prolonged, dynamic effort of composition which had begun in 1784 reached its culmination in December 1786 when he wrote the *Prague* Symphony and the Piano Concerto in C (K. 503). A change then began to come over his creative life. Even allowing for the demands of *Don Giovanni*, it is surely significant that he wrote no more symphonies or concertos for over a year. The public had been content to hum tunes from *Figaro* or to dance to them, and to applaud Mozart as conductor of his own masterpieces or soloist in them, but they brought him neither money nor security. Disillusion began to set in, and was deepened by worry and ill-health over the next two years, during which he composed proportionately much less music and fewer great works. The quality of his inspiration became variable, as in the last two Piano Trios, and the effort sometimes greater, as with the start of the 'Prussian' Quartets.

Even in 1787 the fall in quantity had begun. During the first three months of that year his only substancial works were three concert arias, a set of orchestral dances and the Rondo in A minor for piano. His health was already uncertain and he began to get deeper into debt. Personal grief overtook Mozart when his father became ill and died in May. Shortly before this he had also lost his great friend Count August von Hatzfeld, a gifted musician of exactly his own age, whose death he lamented in the extraordinary letter written on 4 April to his father, during the early stages of the latter's final illness:

> ... I have now made a habit of being prepared in all the affairs of life for the worst. As death, when we come to consider it closely, is the true goal of our existence, I have formed, during the last few years, such close relations with this best and truest friend of mankind, that his image is not only no longer terrifying to me, but is indeed very soothing and consoling.'

Why, in this mood, and in these circumstances, did Mozart turn to the string quintet for the first time in his maturity?

One theory, advanced by Einstein, is that when Frederick William II, an enthusiastic cellist (as we have seen), succeeded Frederick the Great on the throne of Prussia, Mozart had carefully noted that Boccherini was appointed Court composer in January 1786. Einstein conjectures that the latter, after visiting Berlin and

Breslau in 1787, may have gone to Vienna to see his brother who lived there, and that Mozart, having met Boccherini, conceived the plan of composing string quintets with a prominent cello part in order to dedicate them to the royal amateur.

This, however ingenious, is unconvincing if several realistic questions are asked. If Mozart really intended to further his interests by ultimately dedicating six quintets to the King of Prussia, why did he wait over three and a half years between finishing the G minor and starting the D major? Why, during this interval, did he duplicate his intention by composing string quartets for the King? Why, in the end, did he make no effort to bring the quintets to the King's notice? Why is there no mention of such a prolonged, important project in his letters? Moreover, despite the opening of the Quintet in C and a few other passages, the cello enjoys nothing like the melodic prominence that it has in the quartets.

The true reasons are probably simpler. The quintets served two different needs. The unfamiliar medium satisfied Mozart's desire to explore what was virtually a new musical form, and one which, being more powerful than the quartet, but still highly personal, would suit his mood better than either the symphony or the concerto. He may well also have hoped that such novel works might bring in some money. Later, in the spring and summer of 1788, he tried by repeated advertisements to sell on subscription manuscript copies of three quintets (including the arrangement of K. 406) in order to repay one of his many debts to Puchberg.

Even as late as 1787 the medium of the string quintet with two violas had been very little explored. Its origins are rather obscure. It seems to have evolved in the mid-eighteenth century from the divertimento with basso continuo, but very few examples are known before the late 1760s. Such quintets are extant by various composers whose music Mozart knew, including Holzbauer, J. C. Bach, Sammartini and Toeschi. It is generally accepted that the most likely inspiration for the B flat Quintet (K. 174) which Mozart began in the spring of 1773 was a Notturno in C composed by Michael Haydn at Salzburg in the February of that year. It also seems likely that Mozart's later revision of his work and the writing of a new trio and finale was stimulated by a second Quintet, in G, composed by Haydn in the December. (That Mozart had some lasting regard for these quintets is suggested by the fact that he organized and took part in a performance of both at Munich in October 1777.) K. 174 is a rather strange, experimental work, written in the manner of a divertimento, with a mixture of styles, culminating in an elaborate, quasi-contrapuntal finale. He seems to have set some store by it, for in March 1778, when in Munich, he appears to have had the autograph with him and had a copy made to present to the dramatist Baron Otto von Gemmingen-Homberg.

When Mozart decided to arrange for string quintet one of his two wind octets, one wonders why he preferred the C minor (K. 388) of 1782 to the E flat (K. 375) of 1781. On the fair assumption that he made the arrangement early in 1787, he may well have felt that the explosive, near-tragic tone of much of K. 388 was then more congenial to his mood than the contemplative warmth of K. 375. For in terms of general style and the problems of reducing eight wind parts to five strings, there is little to choose between the originals. Although Mozart worked with skill and taste, the result is not altogether happy, mainly because the pungency and varied colour of the four wind instruments cannot be reproduced on strings. Nevertheless, he took full advantage of the enriched tone which the two violas afforded for the inner parts.

He entered the C major Quintet (K. 515) in his catalogue on 19 April, and the G minor (K. 516) on 16 May. Such a close sequence of dates suggests that he conceived the two works as a contrasting pair. For the same duality is found in other mature compositions – the Quartets K. 464 and K. 465 (10 January and 14 January 1785); the Piano Concertos in D minor and C major (K. 467) (10 February and 9 March 1785); the Symphonies in G minor and C major (25 July and 10 August 1788). From this re-current pattern it would appear that two sides of Mozart's character were repeatedly struggling for release – the introspective, verging sometimes on pessimism and despair, alternating with a challenging assertion of resilient optimism and confidence. If this theory is correct, clearly the latter was in the ascendant when he worked on K. 515, whereas the temper of K. 516 suggests that the morbid obsession with death (which is expressed so strongly in the letter quoted on p. 52) overtook him again, aroused perhaps by his father's long illness and foreboding of his imminent end.

The addition of a second viola to the string quartet opened for Mozart, even in his maturity, a new world of expression and experience. Besides tonal and contrapuntal enrichment, it enabled him to plan the music, if he wished, on a much enlarged scale. Moreover, the five instruments could be grouped and regrouped in twos and threes more flexibly than in the quartet. The cello had greater freedom: any instrument could provide extra harmonic support where required. The inner parts could move more freely, provided they did not come too close. To give them the necessary room, Mozart spaced the outer parts more widely. He surely realized that such new opportunities also carried a challenge – to preserve the proportions and balance of all five parts and to maintain their full equality, lest brilliance and concertante effects blur the sharpness of the medium. His genius did not fail him. In all the quintets, inspiration was matched by as high a level of technical accomplishment as in the quartets, and in none more so than in K. 515.

With the remarkable total of 1,149 bars, this is by far the longest of all Mozart's compositions in four movements, and exceeds the other quintets by an average of 400 bars. The two movements of exceptional length are the first and the last, both *allegro*, and both distinguished by wealth of melody, unflagging momentum and a sustained feeling of exhilaration tinged with a seriousness which can perhaps be better felt than analysed. The very opening of the first movement strikes a note of boldness and novelty. A soaring arpeggio of two octaves on the cello is answered by a gruppetto motive on the first violin (used later as a pivot for modulation as in the *allegro* of K. 493), while the other three instruments sustain a powerful throbbing accompaniment which, at a subsequent restatement, is extended from fourteen to seventeen bars. Then, instead of introducing another melody, Mozart repeats the opening, but with the arpeggio on the violin and the answer on the cello – a brilliant stroke. Part of a transitional theme may serve as an example of his skill in writing for all five instruments, and of the warm, romantic harmony characteristic of this quintet:

EX. 16

The principal melodic interest of this *allegro* centres on the contrast between the broad opening theme (which recurs five times, passing through some bewitching changes of key) and the compact second group which weaves its lovely patterns in a whisper that directly echoes the opening of the overture to *Figaro*, and asserts itself throughout the sixty-eight-bar coda.

After this splendid display of outward-looking confidence, the rather cramped opening of the minuet, with its ten-bar phrases and an odd suggestion of uncertain tonality, has a recessive effect. This is deepened by the reflective yet uneasy mood of the unusually long trio (sixty-six bars, equalled only by that of K. 589), and the wavering, chromatic tune of its middle section. Mozart cast the *andante* in the form of a rapt duet between first violin and first viola – floating arabesques of sound with a light, open accompaniment which makes all the more telling such passages as bars 55 to 61 where the dialogue ceases and the five voices coalesce.

The concluding *allegro* recaptures the buoyant, forthright energy of the first, and has much in common, including the pattern of the opening notes, with the finale of K. 465. With 537 bars, this is the longest movement in any of Mozart's instrumental works, and the form, a mixture of rondo and sonata, suits the proportions admirably. The principal subject is treated with wonderful resource at each of its several returns, especially at bar 297 onwards, where it is played in inversion by first violin and second viola, and is simultaneously heard in free imitation on first violin and cello. Most of the other themes are diversified as they recur with brief but most ingenious developments.

This Quintet is a peerless masterpiece, one's admiration for which is only increased by familiarity. Mozart felt it was less important to adhere to the taut thematic processes of the 'Haydn' Quartets than to create a highly organized, yet diverse musical structure on an unparalleled scale. In doing so, he adopted a quasi-symphonic conception which, while stretching the classical style to its limits, yet preserved the spirit of a chamber form. The neglect of this great quintet can only be explained by the fame and more powerful emotional impact of K. 516.

The first movement of K. 516 offers the strongest possible contrast with that of K. 515. Spacious form and a wealth of flowing melodies give place to a compact structure, with few themes, mostly small in compass and built of plaintive, broken phrases. As if to emphasize the prevalent mood, Mozart stays in G minor for the first statement of the second subject with its startling leap of a ninth in its third phrase, which is stretched to a tenth in the closing bars of the movement. Throughout, he keeps the emotional tension as high as possible. To accompany much of both the first and second subjects he gives the inner parts the same sustained throbbing chords which he had used in K. 515, more persistently. He continually passes a phrase from one voice to another in overlapping sequences, or in unrelenting imitation (as in bars 149 to 154). Mozart also favours strongly chromatic progression, leading sometimes to abrupt pauses, of the kind heard in the finale of K. 499, but of a more questioning urgency. Even in such a purely transitional passage as bars 124 to 132, he builds up suspense from a sequence of six six-note phrases, derived from the second subject and played in contrary motion, each time one step lower than the last.

In the minuet, it is the persistence of G minor which makes all the more effective the repetition of the four last bars as the opening of the trio, in G major – so simple yet so moving. Even in the yearning, romantic *adagio*, in E flat, played with mutes throughout, the rapture is uneasy. The little upward-thrusting figure on the second viola at bars 19 and 21, 56 and 58 sends through the music an anticipatory shudder which is not wholly dispelled by such eloquent passages as bars 30, 31 and 69, 70 where the first violin and first viola play in ecstatic imitation over the pulsating demisemiquavers of their partners.

For the G minor *adagio* introductory to the finale, the removal of the mutes heightens the piercing clarity of the dialogue between first violin and cello, which shades off into a lament on the former alone. It rises to a new pitch of almost unbearable tension which dissolves into the 6/8 G major of the controversial *allegro*. Here the first violin predominates, in a spate of lilting melodies, mostly with a light and fascinatingly varied accompaniment. (In only a few passages, such as bars 160 to 172, are the threads more closely woven.) But is this merely a carefree reassertion of Mozart's cheerfulness, or is the apparent gaiety an illusion, hinted at by the ironic echoes of the second subject in the first movement? If the latter, may this not be something more akin to the disconsolate mirth of Penelope's suitors who, while feasting before Odysseus returned to kill them, 'laughed with alien lips' (as Tennyson rendered Homer's vivid phrase)?

Reaction to such a personal work as this Quintet is inevitably subjective. To one hearer it may suggest despair; to another, poignant sadness; to another, passionate defiance, and so on. But whatever the event or experience reflected, the emotions expressed are violent and intense and its purport seems clear. For Mozart himself has provided a clue, in the extraordinary resemblance (which Abert detected) between the G minor *adagio* and the awesome scene in *Die Zauberflöte* when Tamino and Pamina reach the 'Schreckenspforte' – the 'Gates of Dread' – before undergoing the ordeal from which they emerge to light and happiness. The tempo and the plodding 3/4 rhythm are identical; and so, nearly, are both the repeated pizzicato figure in the bass and the line of the melody on the violin.

In this *adagio* Mozart surely reached the climax of a soul-searing, spiritual pilgrimage through which he (unlike Tamino and Pamina) won but an uneasy release. It has been said that Mozart failed to scale the heights in this Quintet because he did not – or could not – compose a finale worthy of the rest. This is absurd. There exists a discarded incipit of a 6/8 finale in G minor[1] which suggests that he decided he could build up a more powerful climax through an *adagio* leading to the kind of ambiguous ending that he favoured in his late works.

The last two string quintets, the D major (K. 593, completed December 1790) and the E flat (K. 614, completed 12 April 1791), differ in character as markedly from each other as each does from either K. 515 or K. 516. This suggests that Mozart conceived the two pairs, despite the gap of three and a half years, as distinctively as he did each of the 'Haydn' Quartets. Nevertheless, K. 593 and K. 614 have various things in common. When published in 1793 by Artaria, each bore on its title page the words 'composto per un amatore ungarese', who has been tentatively identified with Johann Tost, a wealthy cloth merchant and patron of the arts, to whom Haydn dedicated his Quartets Op. 54, 55 and 64. (Since Constanze Mozart stated in 1800 that her husband had worked for Tost, and the name is Hungarian, the identification is possible.) Both quintets continued the eager exploration of the new range of sonority and technique begun in the 'Prussian' Quartets; they are rich in gruppetti, trills and grace-notes such as also proliferate in the two Fantasies for mechanical organ. Both minuets stand third (as in the 'Prussian' Quartets), not second as in the earlier quintets, and gain weight from proximity to the finale. Again, as in the last quartets, each quintet ends with a climactic movement of dynamic energy, tautened by a wealth of counterpoint. Their first and last movements also intensify the capricious quality found in the finale of K. 590 – swift transitions from monophony to polyphony, jerky

[1] Discussed with great insight by Professor Sidney Newman in 'Mozart's G minor Quintet and its Relationship to the G minor Symphony', *Music Review*, November 1956.

rhythms and irregular phrases, and brusque pauses. Both quintets combine pungent conciseness of form with poetic invention and unfailing sureness of touch, all regained since the debacle of mid-1790.

K. 593 is the masterpiece of the least productive year in Mozart's life: in the four months after the completion of K. 590 his sole works were one comic duet and arrangements of Handel's *Alexander's Feast* and *Ode to St Cecilia*. In all Mozart, the structure of the first movement of K. 593 is unique – *larghetto* – *allegro* – *larghetto* – *allegro*. (Perhaps Beethoven remembered it in his Op. 18, no. 6.) The opening, with five spread chords, rising from D to B flat and each answered by the other four voices, seems to strike a mood of questioning. It is intensified by the sixth chord, a chilling diminished seventh on G sharp. The return to the tonic, through the passing warmth of A major, prepares for the assertive, march-like character of the *allegro*, with its predominant dotted quaver rhythms, its open textures contrasted with the vigorous canonic treatment of the main theme in the development.

The thematic material of the rich, pensive *adagio* consists of two alternating groups – a descending, decorated figure (derived from bars 16–17 of the *larghetto*) and yet another rapturous antiphony between first violin and cello, with throbbing inner chords in the manner of K. 515. The minuet is one of Mozart's strongest and most sonorous, built up to a great climax in canon between the two violins and the lower voices. Its solidity is offset by the courtly trio with its high-rising arpeggios, which Mozart revised to make them easier for the cello to play.

As for the 6/8 finale, it almost seems as if he composed the first thirty-five bars with some malice aforethought. Their smooth, chromatic lilt[1] gives no hint that this would harden into one of the most powerful of all Mozart's contrapuntal finales. The opening gives way to a sequence of pungent fugatos interspersed with some astonishing harmonic audacities such as the sudden plunge at bar

[1] The only correct text of this finale, based on the autograph, is found in the Bärenreiter miniature score (No. 11, 1956, ed. by E. F. Schmid) and in the *Neue Mozart Ausgabe*, series VIII (1967). All other editions give the 'zig-zag' alteration made by another hand throughout the autograph, probably in Artaria's publishing house before publication in May 1793. The alteration simplifies performance, but perverts the character of the music. All gramophone recordings of the finale are incorrect.

102 to C after an abrupt pause on B. The movement builds up to this polyphonic climax, comparable to the finale of the *Jupiter*

EX. 17

which resolves through a haunting six-bar chromatic cadence, before the music spins to its dizzy close. This extraordinary finale, with its sudden changes from almost lyrical beauty to the astringent tensions of the minor mode that lurk below the glittering surface, contains the essence of what Einstein aptly called the 'wild, disconsolate mirth' of the whole work.

When Mozart wrote the opening of K. 614, with the violas playing unsupported, he set the mood for one of the most original pieces in all his chamber works. Here, at least in the first three movements, is music of warm, untroubled delight and astonishing vitality, almost spring-like in its luminous self-confidence. In the resilient melody of bars 1 to 3, with the emphatic pointing of three trills, lies the germ of the whole piece. With or without the counterstatement, this motive, so to speak, steals the show. For although there is a second subject (heard, at the recapitulation, most effectively on the first viola), the movement is almost monothematic, right through to the coda where the trilled phrase resounds on the cello. The spirit of the 'Haydn' Quartets lives again, with the added richness of the fifth instrument, in bars 108 to 124, where a trilled derivative hums and hovers from one voice to another, in an airy play of fancy, leading to the recapitulation.

The B flat *adagio* is the very last of Mozart's many essays in variation form. Here he takes only the first part of the simple, two-section melody and weaves round it patterns of poetic fancy, delicately embellished with ornaments akin to those which adorn the contemporaneous Fantasies for mechanical organ. As often in them, a gruppetto figure is very prominent here, echoing through all the voices (bars 89 onwards) while the first violin dwells lingeringly on the theme.

The smooth, descending-octave span of the minuet tune, stated and restated by the violins and violas in different pairs, gains strength in the closing bars, when heard in inversion on the violas. It is music of simple dignity: a worthy crown to the affection and infinite resource which Mozart lavished on the dance-form throughout his thirty-two years of composing. He takes his farewell of the trio in the manner of a *Ländler* (perhaps an echo of the orchestral dances of 1790 and 1791) in which he exploits the peculiar resources of the Quintet to build up a splendid climax. The haunting, sinuous melody is played by the first violin, then repeated with the first viola in unison two octaves below, and finally a third time with the second viola added at the intermediate octave – forty-eight bars of surging sonority over an almost unbroken E flat on the cello, and, at the end, a beautifully harmonized part for the second viola.

While the adjective 'Haydnesque' has been applied, with some justice, to the finale of K. 614, it has really more affinity with the mood and élan of Mozart's own E flat Symphony. Moreover, in K. 614, the warmth of the first three movements gives way to taut, sardonic humour and to a capriciousness fully characteristic of his late chamber works. The chirpy, opening melody consists of two phrases of which the first is clearly derived from the second of the two which commence the first movement. It lends itself admirably to contrapuntal treatment, and from bars 100 to 150 Mozart develops a rattling fugato, beginning in F minor, and based on two principal subjects, each slightly modified from the two phrases of the opening subject. Thereafter, he squeezes every ounce of meaning out of the first of them, by inversion, augmentation and other devices. He uses very simple but brilliantly effective shifts of accompaniment, for instance at bars 286 to 294, with second violin and first viola alone, playing in a gentle cross-rhythm. The very bareness seems to revitalize the hard-worked tune. Even more magical is its reappearance in the coda on the first viola with a soaring answer, again by inversion, played on the first violin.

11. *The Clarinet Quintet and Armonica Quintet*

Though neither of these is equal to the string quintets in style or content, each is unrivalled of its kind and each exemplifies the devotion to the sheer beauty of sound which Mozart cultivated during the last years of his life. The Quintet for clarinet and strings in A (K. 581) was completed on 29 September 1789. It was composed for Anton Stadler, who was one of the leading players of that time, famous in Prague as well as in Vienna where he had been a member of the Imperial Court Orchestra since 1787. For some years previously he had been one of Mozart's circle of musical friends, and was also a freemason. Stadler played with Mozart at masonic gatherings, but seems to have been rather an unstable character who took advantage of financial help which Mozart gave him at a time when he could ill afford it. Yet so disinterested was his friendship that he wrote for him not only this Quintet but also, later, the lovely Concerto which was drafted originally for the basset-horn, on which too Stadler excelled. Mozart took part in the first public performance of the Quintet on 22 December 1789, at a concert given by the Society of Musicians for the benefit of its widows and orphans. In the following April he also played in a private performance to which he invited Puchberg.

Ever since Mozart first heard the clarinet in London when he was eight, he had been fascinated by it, and as his art matured he used it whenever possible in orchestral works and operas. But he had only introduced it twice into chamber music, in K. 452 and K. 498. From his experience in the latter, where it matched so well with the dark tones of the viola, he may well have realized that the clarinet had distinctive possibilities in combination with strings alone. In the Oboe Quartet and the flute quartets, the cool, penetrating quality of the wind instrument had given Mozart little option but to write music conceived partly in concertante style. But the greater range of the clarinet and, especially, the expressive warmth of its middle register made it almost ideal for both blending and contrasting with string tone. In 'Stadler's Quintet', as Mozart himself called it, he achieved another compromise between virtuosity and discourse, although thematic or contrapuntal elaboration is of rather secondary interest.

Contrast, however, there is in plenty throughout. The compact opening melody (remarkably like that of K. 563) is offset by the long-drawn second subject in the dominant, and the delectable modulations of its enlargement by the clarinet. Mozart reserves one moment of pure magic for the restatement of the first subject (just after the double bar, where the clarinet plays it for the first time, with subtle changes in the movement and notes of the violins and viola) and another for the beginning of the short development where the second subject is reshaped by each violin in succession, in C major. The rise and fall of arpeggios on the clarinet shimmer above the semiquavers which pass uninterruptedly through all the strings in turn. Perhaps the most bewitching touch in the recapitulation is the gentle syncopation of the strings that accompanies the second subject restated by the clarinet.

In the *larghetto* (the clear inspiration of the *adagio* in Brahms's Clarinet Quintet), Mozart gave Stadler a quiet arioso of melting loveliness, where the chalumeau register is used with romantic effect, enhanced by all the strings playing with mutes throughout. Their removal for the minuet jerks the music back to the world of an ethereal dance-form with almost perfect equality of all five partners. All the more striking is the bare melancholy of the first trio, in the tonic minor, where the total silence of the clarinet reveals a strict quartet style, and sharpens the hesitancy of the grace-notes. The second trio (a most unusual feature) is a concertante dialogue almost in the manner of a *Ländler* between first violin and clarinet which, for its final flourish, surprisingly picks up the tune from the cello. In the finale, six short variations on a perky melody which seems akin to folksong, Mozart shows again his consummate skill in alternating decoration of a theme with commentary on its essence. The clarinet, prominent especially in the first variation with nimble two-octave skips, is heard little in the second and even less in the third. This, like the second trio, is in A minor: it recaptures and even deepens the mood of unutterable weariness. The tune almost vanishes above the sustained complaint of the viola which is built on repetitions of this joyless phrase:

EX. 18

Allegretto

However Mozart's mood may fluctuate, and however seductive the resources of the clarinet, he never lets it dictate mood or texture, or dominate the ensemble for too long. Sweetness never becomes overripe. As in the more autumnal Clarinet Concerto, sheer beauty of sound takes on a radiant, floating quality which is one of the marks of his late style.

Such is also the character of his last chamber work, the exquisite Quintet for armonica, flute, oboe, viola and cello (K. 617), which he completed on 23 May 1791 for Marianne Kirchgässner, a blind 21-year-old virtuosa from the duchy of Baden who was then in Vienna during a European tour. Mozart's interest in the armonica was not new, for when in London as a child he had heard it played by Marianne Davies, and again in Vienna when on a visit with his father during the summer of 1773. Leopold wrote: 'Herr von Mesmer . . . played to us on Miss Davies's armonica'; and again:

'Do you know that Herr von Mesmer plays on Miss Davies's armonica un-usually well? He is the only person in Vienna who has learnt it and possesses a much finer glass instrument than Miss Davies does. Wolfgang too has played upon it. How I should like to have one!'

The instrument was therefore not strange to Mozart in 1791, but as it is little known today, it deserves a brief description.

The armonica was an improved version of the musical glasses devised and so named in 1762 by Benjamin Franklin. The conventional musical glasses, so widely popular in the eighteenth century, stood upright, each separate, and the player passed moistened fingers quickly over the rims. Seeing how clumsy this was, Franklin revolutionized it by mounting the bells of the glasses horizontally in scale order on a concentric rod, which the player made to revolve by a cranked pedal. Thus chords and scales could be played easily. The compass of about three octaves – from G below middle C upwards – is dictated by the practicable size of the glasses. Their timbre of clear, but piercing sweetness, and its short duration, to some extent govern the style and tempo of the music. All over Europe, up to the 1820s, the armonica enjoyed wide popularity, because of its romantic quality.

Mozart's instinct in choosing instruments which could blend, contrast and support, was faultless. (He took part in a performance of K. 617 on 19 August, probably taking the viola.) The C minor introduction is built of modulating patterns of contrast between the armonica and the other players, moving to a point of tension which is resolved by scale passages melting into C major. The form of the rondo is as transparent as its crystalline texture. Mozart makes marvellous play with a recurring chord-phrase of six descending minim chords, which serve as a hinge for some ravishing modulations, such as the phrases which lead through A flat to the second subject in G. Although the armonica is now found only in museums, the Quintet is far from being a museum piece. Anyone who has heard Bruno Hoffmann's almost uncanny performance of the armonica part on the glasses, or knows his gramophone recording, can testify that this is music of unique beauty in which Mozart's spirit moves on the same plane of serene, ethereal purity as he attained in such other late compositions as the 'Ave verum' or the songs of the Three Boys in *Die Zauberflöte*.

Deep and varied as is our pleasure from Mozart's compositions in larger forms, the bareness and simplicity of the chamber style enable us to share his vision and experience even more keenly –

> 'with an eye made quiet by the power
> of harmony, and the deep power of joy,
> we see into the life of things'.

For through his finest chamber music Mozart sought to communicate what he saw and felt, in sound that is marvellously controlled and shaped by his genius. However intense or disturbing the vision and experience became, the purity of the music was never dimmed by egoism or exaggeration. Such deeply spiritual humanity speaks clearly and unforgettably to the heart.

INDEX OF PRINCIPAL WORKS MENTIONED

INDEX